TO:

FROM:

CONTENTS

(Jokes on you)

(There's no pages numbers)

Why couldn't the prospector buy alcohol?

Because he was a miner!

How does a university measure temperature?

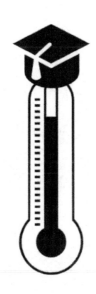

In college degrees

Did you hear that a couple of accountants made a music album?

It was produced by Financial Records

I took my family to the circus the other day...

No one would address the elephant in the room

How does a bird deposit their checks?

They go to the nearest branch

How close was the extension cord race?

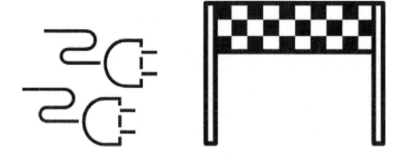

It was down to the wire

I had to take out a loan for my lawn equipment...

It has a great Annual Percentage Rake

What kind of drink does a boxer serve at a party?

Punch

Why doesn't the fisherman have cable anymore?

Because he can just watch the live stream

Why couldn't they sell the Tower of Pisa?

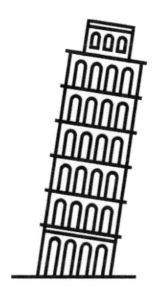

There was a "lien" on it

How many apples did the math equation buy?

Sum

Why was the garbageman self-conscious about his weight?

Because he had a lot of waist

What do you call it when two sky divers go on a date?

Falling in love

What kind of insect goes to church?

A praying mantis

I was driving my cucumber car down a hill when my brakes went out...

Then I was in a pickle

Did you hear about the guy who decided to quit smoking?

Now he has to buy his BBQ

Why do soccer players like spicy food?

It's got a kick to it!

Why does Eminem like Christmas so much?

Because he's great at wrapping

What do you call something good wearing a fake mustache?

A blessing in disguise

You should never throw sodium chloride on a guy after you win a fight…

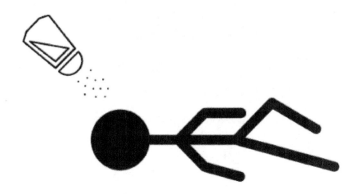

That's just adding in-salt to injury

What does a dad say when you're sick on an airplane?

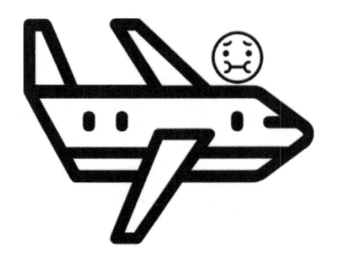

"Looks like you're feeling ABOVE the weather."

Why does red wine know so much gossip?

Because it heard it through the grapevine

Why does dad throw a bag of ice over mom when he's mad at her?

He's giving her the cold shoulder

What did the fast food employee say when supplies were running low?

That's the last straw!

Why can't the car payment make any friends?

Because they're always "a loan"

My buddy Jim and I don't hang out anymore…

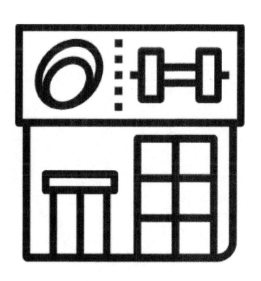

We just never seem to work out

What's a gopher's favorite kind of bread?

Hole wheat

Why did the river update his resume?

He wanted it to be "current"

What does a supportive tree say?

"I'm rooting for you!"

What kind of reindeer lives in the ocean?

A Rudolph-in

How come it's so hard for squirrels to come to a decision?

Because they're always sitting on the fence

Why did the dad throw a deck of cards down a well?

So he could have an ace in the hole

Did you hear about the dog from the streets?

He had a ruff life

What did the baker say after donating to the food bank?

"Don't thank me. It was a piece of cake!"

What does corn say when it's ready to listen?

"I'm all ears!"

How does a pig support his family?

He brings home the bacon

What does a dad say after 24 hours?

I'm going to call it a day

Why do people lose weight when they buy a new car?

Because it costs an arm and leg

What do you call a young potato?

A tater tot-ler

Why do lazy people only draw circles?

Because they love to cut corners

Who's the loneliest of all the cheeses?

Prov-alone

Why do runners always remember everything?

They're always jogging their memory

What did the financially responsible student do to get good grades?

They paid off their "principal"

Why are funerals held before noon?

Because they're always in mourning

What did the doctor say after surgery?

"That's enough out of you!"

My nutritionist says ham has too much sodium…

But I take her opinion with a grain of salt

What did the receptionist say to the invisible man?

The boss can't see you right now

What do you say to a deck of cards that's misbehaving?

"Sit down over there! I'll deal with you later!"

How does a flower ride a bicycle?

It petals

Why do fixed interest rates smell so bad?

Because they never change

Where did the underpaid bowling pins go?

On strike

Why does my wife never turn left?

Because she's always right!

Why did people complain about the party at the tennis player's house?

They were making a lot of racket

You never want to interview with George Foreman...

He really grills you

Why didn't the cattle farmer move to the top of a mountain?

The steaks would be too high

How did the swimmers start an investment fund?

They pooled their money together

I listened to this pirate song the other day...

It had a great hook!

What do you do when a bull charges you?

You pay him!

Why did the elephant buy a car?

It had a big trunk!

Where does an electrician shop?

An outlet mall

What do you call a king who's only a foot tall?

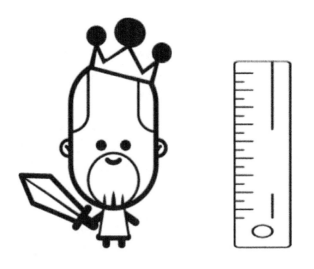

A Ruler

Why does Superman carry a razor?

To shave the day!

How come dad doesn't trust trees?

Because they're shady

What did the dad say to the kitchen counter?

I promise to never take you for granite

Why did the accountant have low self-esteem?

He never gave himself enough "credit"

How did the Medical Plan say goodbye?

Deductible waived

Where does a caveman go with his friends?

The club

Sometimes I think yoga is the cause of all my problems...

But that's a bit of a stretch

How does a good-looking man get paid?

Handsomely

How did the cheese feel after being shredded?

Grate!

How did the contractor chip his tooth?

He was biting his nails

How does Peter Pan get across Lake Michigan?

He takes the "ferry"

Why did the cop pull over the fruit?

They were driving while im-peared

What do you a call a slab of wood with nothing to do?

Board

✓

I joked about stealing my buddy's prosthetic...

I was just pulling his leg

Did you hear about the kangaroo who broke down on the side of the road?

He needed a jump

What's the wind's favorite color?

Blew

How does a chicken get out of an egg?

They use the escape hatch

Did you hear about the accountant who threw a dictionary on the grill?

She was trying to cook the books!

What do you call it when a group of executives falls back during battle?

A corporate retreat

Why do some people become singers?

They do it for the har-money

What's the most common type of bird on a construction site?

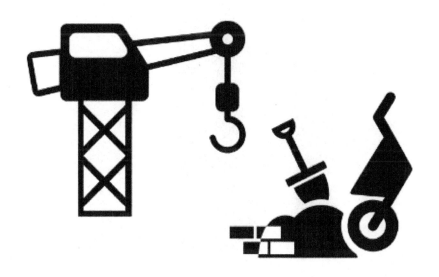

A crane

The leftovers got wrapped up before they could escape...

In other words, their plans were foiled

How come the keyboard didn't want to go on a second date?

He just wasn't her type

Did you hear about the 2 doorbells that got engaged?

sound a doorbell makes

He gave her a nice ring

What's the bounciest of all the seasons?

Spring

Why did the pigs get divorced?

She thought he was a boar

What do you call it when a duck gets a penalty?

A waterfowl

I've seen three looped pieces of string today…

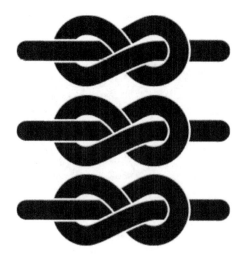

Coincidence, I think knot!

What road do most lions live on?

Mane Street

Why did the tiny bucket go home sick?

He was looking a little pail

What's an investor's favorite religion?

The one with the most prophets

Why was the king sad when the weather cleared up?

His rain was over

Why should you never use an author as a taxi driver?

They always get confused when you tell them to go right

Why did the man get stage fright around steps?

Because of all the stairs

Which metal robbed the jewelry store?

Steel

What do you call a king's chair in the garbage?

Throne away

What type of tree is smaller than your hand?

Palm trees

Did you hear about the well-funded alphabet company?

They had 26 sources of "capital"

What's it called when a Mastercard kicks a field?

Credit score!

You   Me

If you have enjoyed (most of) my jokes, then a review would be greatly appreciated!

If you're feeling generous you can go to www.amazon.com, search for "Extraordinary Dad Jokes", click this book in the search results, scroll down to the Reviews section, and click the "Write a customer review" button.

Thank you so much for reading. I hope you had a great time!

Printed in Great Britain
by Amazon

14438741R00061